CONTENTS

WELCOME

Amanda Van Santen

Amanda Van Santen
RYA Chief Windsurfing Instructor

I'm really excited to be able to guide you through each stage of our RYA Youth Windsurfing Scheme, from your first steps on a board to placing your feet in the straps for the first time.

Welcome to Windsurfing and I look forward to seeing you on the water!

Nick Dempsey

Nick Dempsey
Olympic medallist

I was introduced to windsurfing by my family at the age of 7, at my local lake. For my 8th birthday, I got my first kiddie rig and that was it. I was sailing every day all year round and knew this is what I wanted to do. I finally turned professional at 18.

When the forecast is good, I still get excited and I love the social side. I have made many good friends over the years, both sailing at my local beach and during racing events. I love the sport as much as ever. I don't know why, but maybe because it's different every time and you can improve no matter how good you think you might be and it's never boring. I still have the same dream: winning an Olympic gold medal.

Learning to windsurf is the hardest part. At the start, racing can seem like a scary and complicated subject, but the better you get the more enjoyment you will get from the sport.

Basic racing is simple, easy and virtually anyone who can windsurf can race.

RYA

WINDSURFING is a great sport for all to enjoy

Charlie Metcalfe

UKWA Triple Crown Champion and RYA Trainer

I was introduced to windsurfing while on a two year Youth Training Scheme at an RYA Training Centre on the Isle of Wight. Originally, I enrolled on the course to better my dinghy sailing, but after a short while I discovered windsurfing. I loved it from the first moment I stepped on a board. Windsurfing soon became my new hobby, which became my passion - literally whenever it was windy I could be found at the beach.

Having gained my basic RYA Instructor qualifications, I went on to set up and run a windsurfing centre. This enabled me to teach windsurfing all day every day, which had become my dream.

Having gained further experience teaching and valuable time on the water, I began to enter UKWA Wave sailing and Freestyle competitions and surprised myself by winning!

After working and competing in windsurfing for nearly 10 years, I was invited to do my RYA Trainer's ticket, enabling me to pass my knowledge on to others, by training instructors.

Few of us are lucky enough to start off as natural windsurfers. This logbook and the RYA courses available will guide you through your initial taster, to advanced windsurfing and all the pathways available to you.

Charlie Metcalfe

INTRO

It's all about having that first go, getting wet and having a laugh!

THE RYA YOUTH WINDSURFING SCHEME

The RYA Youth Windsurfing Scheme provides you with an easy and accessible way to progress in this exciting sport, with a certificated course for you to log your progression and recognise your achievements.

RYA YOUTH TRAINING SYLLABUS

The RYA Youth Windsurfing Scheme has been designed to directly relate to the RYA National Windsurfing Syllabus, for ease of use and comparison. Youth Stage 2 is equivalent to Start Windsurfing and Youth Stage 4 equivalent to Intermediate Windsurfing in the National Windsurfing Scheme.

Once completing Stage 4, why stop here? You have all the skills and ability to further your progression through the Advanced Windsurfing course and clinics in the National Windsurfing Scheme. Further details are available in G47, The National Windsurfing Syllabus and Logbook.

If you see ***knowledge of*** generally it means your instructor will talk through some information and then guide you as to where to find out more.

Where you see ***understands***, your instructor will cover the subject in depth and may ask you to demonstrate, with assistance, if necessary.

As you progress through the scheme, your instructor will cover activities and make sure you ***can*** perform them happily, such as tacking and gybing, before they sign your certificate off.

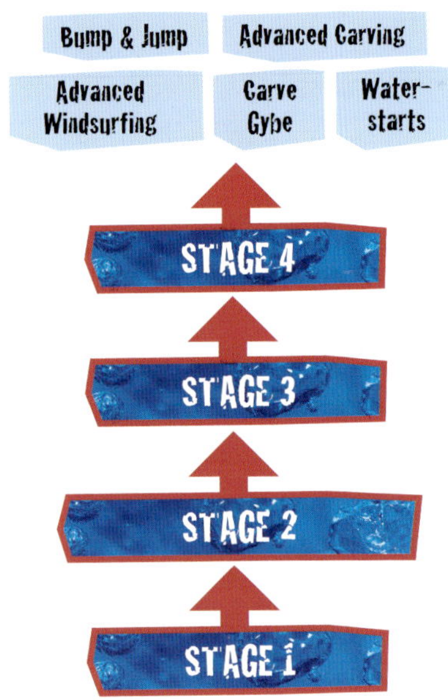

TAKE THE CHALLENGE AND LOG YOUR RESULTS

which are not part of the main certificate, but just fun things for you to try to get your instructor to sign off.

With the Freestyle challenges, we have also provided you with a log at the back of the book so you don't have to just stick to the challenges we have set in each stage!

You will improve your skills and techniques dramatically in all aspects of sailing by just being out on the water on a board and a rig. Furthermore, freestyle and all the skills and moves that exist (and those that are still yet to be discovered) relate to all aspects of windsurfing - from racing to cruising, from flat water inland locations to coastal wavy ones. And one of the best things about freestyle...it has no age or ability restrictions – it's open to everyone.

RYA YOUTH RACING SYLLABUS

Fancy a go at racing?

The RYA Youth Racing Scheme has three badges: Start, Intermediate and Advanced. Having completed your Stage 1 windsurfing badge, you'll be at the right level to begin the Start Racing badge. As you get better, you can progress until you have done your Advanced level, by which time you will be giving the Olympic team a run for their money!

With a network of Team 15 clubs and local events to help introduce you to the fun of racing, you may want to take one step further and progress to achieve your true potential. For further information on racing and Team15 please see page 40.

TRAINING SYLLABUS

YOUTH STAGE 1

This is an ideal first introduction with no prior experience needed. Stage 1 will teach you the basics of getting on the water and sailing the board across the wind and back.

PRACTICAL

LAUNCHING, STARTING AND LANDING...

Can:

- Put on a wetsuit and buoyancy aid NF
- Stand the rig up on land: NF
    - Lean the rig slowly from side to side NF
    - Balance the rig and clap your hands NF
    - Use the wind to fill and empty the sail NF

Has practical understanding of:

(with assistance if required)

- Carrying the board and rig to the water's edge and attaching them together in the water NF
- Getting on the board, using uphaul for balance NF
- Lifting the rig out of the water, establishing the secure position NF

RYA

- Upwind rig recovery
- Lowering the rig, coming ashore and positioning equipment safely NF
- Boom height and adjustment NF

NF

SAILING TECHNIQUES, STANCE AND MANOEUVRES...

Can demonstrate:

- Basic board balancing exercises NF
- Lie, kneel and paddle the board either with or without a partner NF
- Static Steer, progressing onto turning through 180 degrees, either nose or tail through the wind NF
- Get into the sailing position, sailing across the wind, turn the board and return to shore NF
- Control the power in the rig NF
- Stop in control NF
- Attract attention NF
- Demonstrate a basic method of self rescue NF

SAILING BACKGROUND

RIGGING...

Can assist with rigging the board NF

RESCUE TECHNIQUES AND SAFETY...

Has an understanding of:

- Awareness of other water users NF
- The importance of self help and self rescue NF
- Alternative methods of rescue, their uses and limitations NF
- Attracting attention NF

SAILING THEORY...

- Can name basic components of the board and rig NF
- Has knowledge of the wind direction NF

EQUIPMENT...

- Has knowledge and knows the importance of newcomers' boards and rigs (including size and suitability) and wearing a wetsuit and buoyancy aid NF

OTHER ASPECTS AND OPTIONS...

- The Stage 2 course NF
- Regular activity (clubs/Team 15) NF
- An introduction to the racing syllabus and the Start Racing certificate NF
- Freestyle as a way to build on our ability and opportunity to log our progress NF

By the end of this first certificate, you should be able to launch your equipment in the water and sail the board, returning to the original point on the shore by sailing or combining a method of self rescue

Rigging stick can be used as an introduction to sections of the above. To sign the elements a rig must be used.

TAKE A CHALLENGE...

- Dragging a foot in the water whilst sailing NF
- Clapping whilst sailing
- Starting from the beach as a group: sail or paddle around a buoy and return to the beach and see who gets back first. Perhaps even get into teams and make the challenge into a relay!!

RYA Youth

WINDSURFING SCHEME

STAGE 1

This is to certify that

Arron Burgess

has successfully completed all the requirements of this stage within the RYA Youth Windsurfing Scheme.

Signed Sarah North
(Principal / Chief Instructor)

Of Portomynna Palace
(RYA Recognised Training Centre)

~~Tidal~~ / Non Tidal* (*please delete as appropriate)

Date 15/7/16

YOUTH STAGE 2

During your Stage 2 course, your instructor will teach you the practical skills to get you sailing around, practising tacking and gybing, enabling you to make progression towards and away from the wind. It is assumed that before taking this course, you have mastered the practical skills and background knowledge required for the Stage 1 course.

PRACTICAL

LAUNCHING, STARTING AND LANDING...

Has practical understanding of:
(with assistance if required)

- Launching the board and rig together NF
- Return to shore in control and removing the board and rig from the water NF
- Leaving the board and rig on the shore safely NF

SAILING TECHNIQUES, STANCE AND MANOEUVRES...

Can:

- Sail the board across the wind, turning between two points NF

Steering

- Steer the board towards the wind NF
- Steer the board away from the wind NF
- Sail the board between two points making ground towards and away from the wind NF

Upwind and Tacking

- Sailing upwind NF
- Tacking on the move to change direction NF

Downwind and gybing

- Sailing downwind NF
- A basic non-planing carve gybe on the move NF

SAILING BACKGROUND

RIGGING...

Has practical understanding of:

- Basic rigging, de-rigging and storage requirements NF
- The names and the uses of the main parts of the board and rig NF
- Boom height and adjustment NF

Can:

- Tie a figure of eight knot NF
- Tie a round turn and two half hitches NF
- Tie a reef knot NF

RESCUE TECHNIQUES AND SAFETY...

Has an understanding of:

- Safety equipment and essential spares NF

SAILING CONDITIONS...

Has basic knowledge of:

- The effects of onshore, cross-shore and offshore winds on a sailing area NF
- Weather: sources and a basic interpretation, effect on sailing area NF
- Tide: sources and a basic interpretation; effect on sailing area (if applicable) NF
- The Beaufort Scale NF
- Personal limitations NF

SAILING THEORY...

Understands:

- The points of sailing NF
- The 'no- go zone' and its effect on the means of sailing upwind NF
- Terms - windward/leeward, upwind/downwind, port/starboard NF

Has knowledge of:

- The rules of the road – power gives way to sail, port versus starboard, overtaking vessel and windward vessel NF

EQUIPMENT...

Has knowledge of and understands the importance of:

- The range of suitable clothing and accessories NF
- Types of wetsuit NF

OTHER ASPECTS AND OPTIONS...

- The Stage 3 course NF
- Opportunities for regular practice NF
- T15 and/or club activity NF

By the end of this stage, you should have had a basic introduction to the background knowledge of windsurfing and have combined this with the practical skills gained, to sail around a course, practising tacking and gybing, making progress upwind and downwind, and understanding when to tack and gybe. A static turn downwind is acceptable should the conditions be challenging.

TAKE A CHALLENGE...

- Try kneeling whilst sailing
- Rig 180s
- Starting and finishing from the beach, sail around a three buoy, downwind slalom course. If you are really up for a challenge, combine this with the challenge in Stage 1 – start afloat between two buoys with a ten second warning before the GO!

THE RYA YOUTH WINDSURFING CHALLENGE IMPROVE YOUR BOARD SKILLS

RYA

RYA Youth WINDSURFING SCHEME

STAGE 2

This is to certify that

Arron Burgess

has successfully completed all the requirements of this stage within the RYA Youth Windsurfing Scheme.

Signed Sarah North
(Principal / Chief Instructor)

Of Portomyriaa Palace
(RYA Recognised Training Centre)

~~Tidal~~ / Non Tidal* (*please delete as appropriate)

Date 15/7/16

YOUTH

STAGE 3

Once you have mastered the practical skills and knowledge required in Stage 2, it's time to hook in and hang on.......! Using the RYA's Fastfwd coaching formula, your instructor will help you to correctly set up your board and rig, enhance your stance on all points of sailing and introduce basic harnessing techniques in stronger winds.

PRACTICAL

Has developed an understanding of, and can apply the Fastfwd Formula (Vision, Trim, Balance, Power and Stance) to:

LAUNCHING, STARTING AND LANDING...

Can:

- Carry and launch the board and rig together (alone or in pairs) NF
- Come ashore under control and landing in stronger winds
- Remove the board and rig from the water and leave the board and rig securely ashore

BEACHSTARTING...

Can:

- Recover the rig NF
- Control the board and rig together in the shallows NF
- Get onto the board in shallow water and sail away using a beachstart NF
- Beachstart in a variety of wind directions

SAILING TECHNIQUES, STANCE AND MANOEUVRES...

Can demonstrate the basic principles of the following:

- Improved stance on all points of sailing
- Gust control
- Altering the daggerboard to suit conditions and points of sailing
- Maintaining sailing line
- Improved steering using body weight and the rig NF
- Correct sail adjustment on all points of sailing

Harness

- A basic understanding of using the harness to improve, trim, balance, power and stance
- Basic harness techniques NF NF
- Harness - Correct harness adjustment NF
- Hooking in and out NF

Tacking

- Maintaining speed and flowing movement in stronger winds
- Better use of the rig and weight control during:
  - Preparation and approach
  - Initiation

Gybing

- Maintaining speed and flowing movement in stronger winds
- Developing body position throughout the gybe
- Better use of the rig and weight control during:
  - Preparation and approach
  - Initiation
  - Rig rotation, timing and foot change
- Improving the gybe and downwind sailing, sailing clew first and steering on a run
- Completing the non-planing carve gybe using correct weight distribution in a variety of conditions, maintaining speed and power

YOUTH STAGE 3

SAILING BACKGROUND

RIGGING...

Can demonstrate the basic principles of the following:

- Choosing, rigging and de-rigging a sail suitable for the prevailing conditions NF
- Basic sail tuning
- Harness lines, correct positioning and adjustment NF

RESCUE TECHNIQUES AND SAFETY...

Has understanding of:

- The importance of self help and self rescue NF
- Safety equipment and essential spares
- Awareness of other water users NF

SAILING CONDITIONS...

Has basic knowledge of:

- Sea state in relation to the wind and tide
- Spotting deteriorating weather from visual sky signs
- Tides - springs/neaps, tidal streams, strength and visual signs NF
- Choosing a safe sailing location

SAILING THEORY...

Has understanding of:

- Rules of the road - power gives way to sail, port versus starboard, overtaking vessel and windward vessel NF
- Wind awareness and its effect NF
- Parts of a board and rig NF
- The daggerboard and its effect; sailing with/without, all points of sailing
- Centre of Effort and Centre of Lateral Resistance and their effect NF
- The 'no go zone' and its effect on the means of sailing upwind NF

Having completed Stage 3, you should be able to, with assistance, correctly set up your board and rig to the conditions, sail on all points, understanding when to tack and gybe, with and without the daggerboard (understanding its uses and limitations).
You should also have a basic understanding of applying the Fastfwd Formula to aspects of your sailing, and by using an effective stance, show basic harnessing techniques.
The skills and knowledge gained should mean you can now sail safely and in control.

EQUIPMENT...

Understands the importance of:

- Board types, uses and limitations NF
- The relationship between board volume and body weight NF
- Suitable clothing, accessories and seasonal suitability NF
- The advantages and disadvantages of different types of windsurfing equipment
- Board volume in relation to wind strengths, uses and limitations
- Types of harness and harness lines available
- Equipment - purchase, transport, storage and maintenance

OTHER ASPECTS AND OPTIONS...

- The Stage 4 course
- Becoming an assistant instructor and volunteering at your local club or training centre
- Pathway and equipment options in relation to it

TAKE A CHALLENGE...

- Clew-first sailing
- Body 360s
- Sailing around a triangle without the daggerboard
- Ask your instructor to lay a course in the shape of a triangle starting from the beach see who can sail around and back first. Make it really exciting and have a start line between a boat and a buoy or two, counting down for a start.

THE RYA YOUTH WINDSURFING CHALLENGE IMPROVE YOUR BOARD SKILLS

RYA Youth
WINDSURFING SCHEME

STAGE 3

STICK YOUR STAGE 3 CERTIFICATE HERE

This is

has successfully completed all the requirements of this stage within the RYA Youth Windsurfing Scheme.

Signed

Of

Tidal / Non Tidal* (*please delete as appropriate)

Date

RYA

YOUTH STAGE 4

Blasting around and getting in the footstraps is what this next stage is all about! Having completed Stage 4 you should have the confidence and ability to tack and gybe and sail in your harness with an introduction to basic footstrap technique. Passing this certificate is the natural entry point into the advanced courses in the National Windsurfing Scheme.

It is assumed that before taking this course, you have mastered the practical skills and background knowledge required for the Stage 3 course.

PRACTICAL

Has developed an understanding of, and can apply the Fastfwd Formula (Vision, Trim, Balance, Power and Stance) to:

LAUNCHING, STARTING AND LANDING...

Can:

- Carry and launch the board and rig together
- Use improved uphauling in planing conditions
- Stop under control
- Land and come ashore under control

SAILING TECHNIQUES, STANCE AND MANOEUVRES...

Can:

- Effectively use the board and sail to encourage planing
- Demonstrate improved harness technique and line adjustment for the conditions
- Effectively refine stance when hooked in, for the conditions, on all points of sail
- Cope with gusts and lulls

Footstraps

- Can correctly adjust the footstraps
- Understands basic footstrap technique

- Make use of both footstraps
- Maintain position in relation to the wind
- Apply basic foot and toe pressure

Improved steering

- Tacking in stronger winds, maintaining speed into the turn and flowing movements
- Gybing in stronger winds, maintaining speed and power, and demonstrating an ability to rotate the rig
- Daggerboard use, sailing with/without; on all points of sailing

SAILING BACKGROUND

RIGGING...

Can:

- Rig and de-rig
- Tune equipment to suit conditions
- Correct adjustment of footstraps
- Tie a bowline

RESCUE TECHNIQUES AND SAFETY...

Has understanding of:

- Towing another board and sailor, tow lines and methods of attachments
- Actions to be taken in potential emergency situations
- Alternative methods of self rescue

SAILING CONDITIONS...

Has an understanding of:

- Where to obtain a weather forecast,
- Basic prediction of a synoptic chart
- Comparison with local conditions and expected changes
- Predicting changes in wind direction during a low pressure system
- Wind and weather associated with a high pressure system
- Using a tide table to obtain the time of high and low water, predicting expected changes and fastest flow, recognising dangerous tidal areas
- The effects of spring and neap tides
- Choosing a safe sailing venue considering the above, weather forecast and tidal information

SAILING THEORY...

Understands basic theory of:

- Apparent wind and its effect on the sail as speed changes
- Sailing upwind without a daggerboard
- How a sail works
- Fins and their effects on performance

EQUIPMENT...

Has understanding of:

- The advantages and disadvantages of different types of windsurfing equipment
- Lower volume boards, their uses and limitations
- Board volume in relation to wind strengths
- Types of harness and harness lines available
- Equipment care and storage
- Equipment: purchase, transport, storage and maintenance

OTHER ASPECTS AND OPTIONS...

- The Advanced courses and clinics in the RYA National Scheme (Page38)

Having completed the Stage 4 certificate, you should be able to correctly set up your equipment for the conditions, enabling you to show a confident ability to tack and gybe, sail in your harness and show basic footstrap technique. Passing the Stage 4 certificate is also the natural entry point for the advanced courses in the National Windsurfing Scheme.

TAKE A CHALLENGE...

- Clew-first beachstarts
- Helicopter tack
- This will make you dizzy!! Ask your instructor to lay a course with some buoys, setting a challenge to complete a certain number of tacks or gybes on the upwind and downwind legs. Adding a start line with a count down of 2 minute, 1 minute, GO start, will increase the challenge!

THE RYA YOUTH WINDSURFING CHALLENGE IMPROVE YOUR BOARD SKILLS

RYA

RYA Youth

WINDSURFING SCHEME

STAGE 4

This is to certify that

STICK YOUR STAGE 4 CERTIFICATE HERE

has success… tage
within the… Scheme.

Signed

Of

Tidal / Non Tidal* (*please delete as appropriate)

Date

RACING SYLLABUS

START RACING

RACING BACKGROUND

RACING PATHWAYS AND STRUCTURE...

Has knowledge of:

- Team 15 interclub challenges
- Scheme structure
- Equipment used in RYA System

RACING THEORY

RACING KNOWLEDGE...

Has an understanding of:

- A racing start line
- The port/starboard rule
- A simple starting sequence
- Being close to the start line on the gun
- Wind shadows
- The legs of a course i.e. beat, reach, run

WIND/WEATHER/TIDE...

Can:

- Obtain and understand a simple weather forecast
- Select the correct rig and equipment for the conditions
- Understand high and low tide

PRE-RACE PREPARATION

EQUIPMENT PREPARATION...

Has an understanding of:

- Boom height
- How to prevent boom slippage
- Tightening battens
- Setting a sail for the conditions

BOARD AND KIT CARE...

Can:

- Carry out a visual inspection, (looking for cracks, holes)
- Avoid damage, stones, rough surfaces

HEALTH AND NUTRITION...

Has knowledge of:

- Food as a fuel
- Keeping hydrated

FITNESS...

Has knowledge of:

- The physical demands of racing
- Performing basic injury prevention i.e. warm up, cool down, stretching

TECHNIQUE

STARTING...

Can demonstrate the basics of:

- Getting near the start line on gun
- Stopping and holding position

SPEED...

Can demonstrate the basics of:

- Developing stance
- Trimming the board upwind and downwind

Can demonstrate the basics of :

- Faster tacks and gybes
- Gybing around a mark, entering wide and exiting tight

Can demonstrate the basics of :

- Keeping clear wind
- Tacking in correct place for windward marks

Once you have completed Start Racing, you should be able to race around a course in a small fleet and understand the starting procedure and course configuration.

TAKE A CHALLENGE...

- **Take part in an interclub event**

THE RYA YOUTH WINDSURFING CHALLENGE IMPROVE YOUR BOARD SKILLS

RYA Youth

WINDSURFING SCHEME

START RACING

This

STICK YOUR START RACING CERTIFICATE HERE

has successfully completed all the requirements of this stage within the RYA Youth Windsurfing Scheme.

Signed

(Principal/Chief Instructor)

Of

(RYA Recognised Training Centre)

Tidal / Non Tidal* (*please delete as appropriate)

Date

INTERMEDIATE RACING

RACING BACKGROUND

RACING PATHWAYS AND STRUCTURE...

Has knowledge of:

- RYA squad structures
- Equipment used in International Youth & Junior Systems
- UKWA regional racing
- Understanding role of RYA and UKWA

RACING THEORY

RACING KNOWLEDGE...

Has an understanding of:

- Racing courses
- The windward/leeward rule
- A standard starting sequence including flags
- Being on the start line on the gun
- Taking penalties (360)
- Hailing protest
- Clear air and positioning at the start

WIND/WEATHER/TIDE...

Can:

- Obtain, understand and use a weather forecast
- Select the correct settings for the conditions
- Understand tides and timings of high and low water
- Spot and react to gusts

RYA

PRE-RACE PREPARATION

EQUIPMENT PREPARATION...

Has an understanding of:

- Rig settings for different conditions
- Knowing when to change up/down sail size
- Adjustable harness lines and setting the lines in the correct position
- Legal sail numbers and positioning

BOARD AND KIT CARE...

Can:

- Ensure daggerboard works easily and effectively
- Keep fin and daggerboard in good condition

HEALTH AND NUTRITION...

Has an understanding of:

- Using food to enhance performance
- Aware of the effects of dehydration

FITNESS...

Has knowledge of:

- Awareness of the requirement for physical fitness and training for racing
- Regular use of injury prevention techniques, warm up/cool down and stretching

TECHNIQUE

STARTING...

Can demonstrate the basics of:

- Practise reversing
- Controlling board in tight situations
- Manoeuvring under control

SPEED...

Can demonstrate the basics of:

- Achieving the correct pointing angle
- Using railing upwind
- Rapid and efficient daggerboard movement relative to leg of course
- Using the harness
- Beginning to develop pumping technique

TURNING TECHNIQUES...

Can demonstrate the basics of:

- Faster gybing in stronger winds
- Accelerating out of tacks and resuming pointing angle

TACTICS AND STRATEGY...

Has knowledge and understanding of:

- Leeward mark roundings
- Deciding which side of the beat to go up and an awareness that the two sides may not be equal
- Spotting and using wind shifts on the upwind leg

The knowledge and practical experience gained by completing the Intermediate Racing Certificate should enable you to race around a course, make race decisions based upon rules and strategy, with an awareness of other competitors.

TAKE A CHALLENGE...

- **Attend the RYA Zone championships**

THE RYA YOUTH WINDSURFING CHALLENGE IMPROVE YOUR BOARD SKILLS

RYA

Youth

WINDSURFING SCHEME

INTERMEDIATE RACING

This

STICK YOUR INTERMEDIATE RACING CERTIFICATE HERE

has successfully completed all the requirements of this stage within the Racing Syllabus.

Signed ....

(Racing Coach Level 2)

Of ....

(Club / Centre)

Tidal / Non Tidal* (*please delete as appropriate)

Date ....

ADVANCED RACING

RACING BACKGROUND

RACING PATHWAYS AND STRUCTURE...

Has knowledge of:

- UK racing structure/class associations and equipment
- Class rules
- National racing
- Understanding the role of qualification routes for RYA Zone/National Squads

RACING THEORY

RACING KNOWLEDGE...

Has an understanding of:

- The use of racing courses
- The basics of RRS (Racing Rules of Sailing) part 1
- The basics of RRS part 2

WIND/WEATHER/TIDE...

Can:

- Understand and show awareness of the sea breeze effect
- Predict conditions from simple weather forecasts
- Demonstrate an awareness of the relevance and effect of tidal streams

PRE-RACE PREPARATION

EQUIPMENT PREPARATION...

Has an understanding of:

- Rig settings using adjustable outhaul and downhaul

RYA

- How to set a sail for maximum performance in all conditions
- Essential spares for competition
- Ensuring equipment is class legal and complies with current class rules

BOARD AND KIT CARE...

Can:

- Maintain foils and hull in good condition
- Demonstrate knowledge of basic board repair

HEALTH AND NUTRITION...

Has an understanding of:

- The use of sports drinks
- The effective use of food as a performance enhancer

FITNESS...

Has knowledge of:

- Establishing a basic fitness regime for windsurfing
- Incorporating body weight training into fitness programme

TECHNIQUE

STARTING...

Can demonstrate the basics of:

- Developing a starting plan
- Creating gaps on the start line using board control
- Accelerating and predicting the gun to ensure speed at start

SPEED...

Can demonstrate the basics of:

- Using a tuning partner to test speed and height upwind

- Keeping a constant and smooth angle upwind
- Mast track adjustment
- Solid pumping technique both up and downwind
- Effective stance and control downwind

TURNING TECHNIQUES...

Can demonstrate the basics of:

- Carve gybing
- Faster 360 penalty turns

TACTICS AND STRATEGY...

Has knowledge and understanding of:

- Pre-race plan, checking course and making a decision as to which way to go
- Recognition and awareness of wind shifts
- Bearing away in a gust downwind

An Advanced Racing certificate means you have the skills to prepare yourself for, and race around a course, in a large fleet and make decisions, using rules, tactics and strategy both in regards to own sailing and that of the fleet.

TAKE A CHALLENGE...

- **Enter the RYA Youth & Master Championships**

THE RYA YOUTH WINDSURFING CHALLENGE IMPROVE YOUR BOARD SKILLS

Youth
WINDSURFING SCHEME

ADVANCED RACING

This

STICK YOUR ADVANCED RACING CERTIFICATE HERE

has successfully completed all the requirements of this stage within the Racing Syllabus.

Signed ....

Of ....

Tidal / Non Tidal* (*please delete as appropriate)

Date ....

TRY SOMETHING DIFFERENT

Here are 10 freestyle skills to get you started.

They get slightly more advanced as you move from first to last. Try each move in light winds first and as you get better, perhaps start trying them in a little more wind!!

Having fun and trying new skills on your board is an essential way to helping you progress in your windsurfing and onto more advanced skills. For example, sailing 'front to sail' builds on your ability to balance on the board, increase wind awareness and forms the foundations for other moves such as helicopter tacks, upwind and downwind 360s, and even spocks!

Perhaps make some moves up yourself or with friends and let us know how they are helping you progress and have fun with your windsurfing.

THE 10 FREESTYLE SKILLS...

1 Lifting a foot / dragging a foot in the water

- Great for progressing onto beachstarts, waterstarts and general control of board, rig and yourself!

2 Kneeling / sitting / lying down whilst sailing

- Good practice exercise for beach starting and water starting
- Enhances rig control by holding the foot of sail and mast only!
- Gets a person moving on the board rather then being 'stuck' to it

3 Switch stance sailing

- Ties in with more advanced moves like duck tacks, push tacks and 'sliding' manoeuvres

4 Clapping / pirouettes

- Teaches nature of rig balance and helps with 'ducking' of rig
- Emphasises the use of your head and being nimble on our feet

5 Rig 180s / rig 360s (ducking the rig)

- Gives great rig confidence and is vital for a high level of rig control
- Great for progressing onto duck gybes, clew-first sailing

6 Clew-first sailing / clew-first beachstarts

- Great for gybe exits (non-planing and planing)
- Another vital skill to help give a high level of rig control
- Helps progression for advanced skills such as grubbies

7 Sailing backwards / sailing on the nose

- Helps with rig and board control
- Progression onto willyskippers and stylish launching/landing at an awkward location!

8 Body and rig 360

- Introduces concept of 'front to sail' and is great for nimble footwork!
- Good building blocks for upwind 360s, backwind gybes, monkey and reverse monkey gybes

9 Sailing 'front to sail'

- Gives a greater understanding of rig control
- Pinnacle manoeuvre leading to better tacks, helicopter tacks, upwind 360s, tack and gybe variations

10 Helicopter tack

- Try clew first, switch stance (or both!) variations
- Combines a lot of the previous moves and skills

WHAT'S NEXT?

ADVANCING YOUR SKILLS

Once you have completed Stage 4, the natural progression is the Advanced Course and Clinics within the RYA National Windsurfing Scheme. For more information see the National Windsurfing Scheme Syllabus and Logbook (G47).

The main advanced course concentrates on core sailing techniques, helping you to sail in a variety of conditions by progressing wind skills into those needed for blasting control.

Waterstarting, Planing Carve Gybes, Bump and Jump and Advanced Carving Skills are additional clinics that fit neatly around the main advanced course. Each clinic can be taught as part of a course, as a single clinic or as an ongoing learning experience.

RYA

STARBOARD

TEAM 15...

Team 15 is a nationwide network of clubs where the coolest windsurfers aged 15 or under get together every week, learn new skills and have a great time.

Who says you can't be safe and have fun? All Team15 clubs operate at recognised RYA Windsurfing Centres or RYA Affliated Clubs.

Getting into the T15 clubbin' scene is easy, it doesn't cost the earth and if you're just starting out, we even provide all the equipment. Whether you windsurf already or are just taking your first go – T15 is the place to be.

Once you are totally hooked, you'll want to aim to get into your T15 club team: A specially selected team of 15, who represent their club at four annual inter-club events.

For further information check it out online: www.team15.org.uk.

T15

www.team15.org.uk

"Team 15 is a great way to meet new friends. Within two times of going to the club I had lots of new friends. The coaches are amazing and it's really laid back and enjoyable."

Joe, 13, Team Astbury

FANCY A GO AT RACING?...

With a network of Team 15 clubs and local events to help introduce you into how much fun racing is, you may want to take one step further to progress and achieve your true potential.

Open training sessions are organised locally, provided by expert coaches and delivered at clubs across the country. Following this training, you can apply for RYA Zone Squad or National Squad depending on your age and ability.

You may also want to consider attending your local RYA Zone or Home Country Championship – these usually take place on the last weekend in September each year and enable young sailors to show off their skills under the watchful eye of RYA High Performance Managers and Coaches.

Zone Squads are designed to feed talented sailors into the RYA National Junior Squad programme, enabling them to develop and ultimately succeed at various championships.

For more information and details, check out the National Junior Squad section of the RYA Website: www.rya.org.uk or the RYA Racing Department direct.

BECOMING AN INSTRUCTOR-INSTRUCTOR PATHWAY...

With windsurfing having grabbed your attention you may wish to pass the skills you have learnt from this infectious sport to others. You can start your progression on the instructional ladder once you have achieved your Stage 3 certificate. Once you have this, you could become an Assistant Instructor at your local training centre. Turning 16, you may choose to become a fully qualified RYA Start Windsurfing Instructor.

Full details on becoming an instructor are available on the RYA Training Website: www.ryatraining.org

INTRODUCING RACING INTO YOUR CENTRE OR CLUB

If you have basic racing experience or would like to be given the opportunity to learn basic race coaching techniques, the Racing Instructor course will cover instructional techniques afloat and ashore. Candidates do need to be a minimum of a Start Windsurfing Instructor to attend this course or gain this qualification.

Race Coaching Pathway

Playing a part in helping talented windsurfers to progress and achieve their goals in our fantastic sport is a great feeling. The RYA race coach schemes allow individuals with knowledge and experience the chance to gain skills in order to progress in the world of coaching. Coaches play a massive role in the RYA programmes from regional junior to Olympic level and if you feel that this is a route that you would like to pursue full details are available on the RYA Website www.rya.org.uk

DATE...	LOCATION...	BOARD...	RIG...	CONDITIONS...	ACTIVITY...

RYA

DATE...	LOCATION...	BOARD...	RIG...	CONDITIONS...	ACTIVITY...

LOGGIN'

NOTES

RYA Membership

Promoting and Protecting Boating

www.rya.org.uk

RYA Membership

Promoting and Protecting Boating

The RYA is the national organisation which represents the interests of everyone who goes boating for pleasure. The greater the membership, the louder our voice when it comes to protecting members' interests. Apply for membership today, and support the RYA, to help the RYA support you.

Benefits of Membership

- Special members' discounts on a range of products and services including boat insurance, books, charts, DVD's and class certificates
- Access to expert advice on all aspects of boating from legal wrangles to training matters
- Free issue of Certificates of Competence, increasingly asked for by everyone from overseas governments to holiday companies, insurance underwriters to boat hirers
- Access to the wide range of RYA publications, including the quarterly magazine
- Third Party insurance for windsurfing members
- Regular offers in RYA Magazine

...and much more

JOIN NOW

Membership form opposite or join online at **www.rya.org.uk**
Visit our website for information, advice, members' services and web shop

IT'S ALL ABOUT YOU AND THE BOATING YOU DO

RYA MEMBERSHIP APPLICATION

RYA Be part of it

One of boating's biggest attractions is its freedom from rules and regulations. As an RYA member you'll play an active part in keeping it that way, as well as benefiting from free expert advice and information, plus discounts on a wide range of boating products, charts and publications.

To join the RYA, please complete the application form below and send it to The Membership Department, RYA, RYA House, Ensign Way, Hamble, Southampton, Hampshire SO31 4YA. You can also join online at www.rya.org.uk, or by phoning the membership department on +44 (0) 23 8060 4159. Whichever way you choose to apply, you can save money by paying by Direct Debit. A Direct Debit instruction is on the back of this form.

	Title	Forename	Surname	Gender	Date of Birth
Applicant 1					/ /
Applicant 2					/ /
Applicant 3					/ /
Applicant 4					/ /

E-mail Applicant 1 ______ Address ______

E-mail Applicant 2 ______

E-mail Applicant 3 ______

E-mail Applicant 4 ______ Post Code ______

Home Tel ______ Day Time Tel ______ Mobile Tel ______

Save money by completing the Direct Debit form overleaf

Type of membership required (Tick Box)

- ☐ **Junior (0-11)** Annual rate £5 or **£5 if paying by Direct Debit**
- ☐ **Youth (12-17)** Annual rate £14 or **£11 if paying by Direct Debit**
- ☐ **Under 25** Annual rate £25 or **£22 if paying by Direct Debit**
- ☐ **Personal** Annual rate £43 or **£39 if paying by Direct Debit**
- ☐ **Family*** Annual rate £63 or **£59 if paying by Direct Debit**

Please number up to three boating interests in order, with number one being your principal interest

☐ Yacht Racing	☐ Yacht Cruising	☐ Dinghy Racing	☐ Dinghy Cruising
☐ Personal Watercraft	☐ Sportboats & RIBs	☐ Windsurfing	☐ Motor Boating
☐ Powerboat Racing	☐ Canal Cruising	☐ River Cruising	

** Family Membership: 2 adults plus any under 18s all living at the same address. Prices valid until 30/9/2011 One discount voucher is accepted for individual memberships, and two discount vouchers are accepted for family membership.*

IMPORTANT In order to provide you with membership benefits the details provided by you on this form and in the course of your membership will be maintained on a database. If you do not wish to receive information on member services and benefits please tick here ☐. By applying for membership of the RYA you agree to be bound by the RYA's standard terms and conditions (copies on request or at www.rya.org.uk)

Signature ______ Date / / Source Code ______ Joining Point Code ______

PAY BY DIRECT DEBIT – AND SAVE MONEY

Instructions to your Bank or Building Society to pay by Direct Debit

Please fill in the form and send to:

Membership Department, Royal Yachting Association, RYA House, Ensign Way, Hamble, Southampton, Hampshire SO31 4YA.

Name and full postal address of your Bank/Building Society

To the Manager Bank/Building Society

Address

Postcode

Name(s) of Account Holder(s)

Branch Sort Code __ __ – __ __ – __ __

Bank/Building Society Account Number

Originator's Identification Number

9 5 5 2 1 3

DIRECT Debit

RYA Membership Number (For office use only)

Instructions to your Bank or Building Society

Please pay Royal Yachting Association Direct Debits from the account detailed in this instruction subject to the safeguards assured by The Direct Debit Guarantee. I understand that this instruction may remain with the Royal Yachting Association and, if so, details will be passed electronically to my Bank/Building Society.

Signature(s)

Date: D D / M M / Y Y Y Y